Chasing Sunshine:

Finding My Way Back To The Light

By Regina Sunshine Robinson

Chasing Sunshine

Chasing Sunshine: Finding My Way Back To The Light
Published 2024 by Regina Sunshine Global Network LLC

Copyright 2024 by Regina Sunshine Robinson

Cover Design by Darshawne Wickerson
Edited by Charlotte Ehney

ISBN: 979-8-9862575-4-9 Paperback
ISBN: 979-8-9862575-5-6 Ebook

Bible references quoted from the English Standard Version, the New International Version, the New Living Translation Version, and the New King James Version from www.biblegateway.com.

For information:
Regina Sunshine Global Network, LLC
www.ReginaSunshine.com

Dedication

I dedicate this book to the memory of my mother, Geraldine Alford Gore. She was the Original Sunshine and Love Personified. It has been hard living in a world without her but her words to me continue to push me forward in purpose.

Thank you, Mama, for laying a solid foundation for me to return to when the whole world was spinning. I will not give up. I will live, really live. And I will continue to make you proud.

It is never goodbye for us…only see you later.

Regina

Table of Contents

Introduction Part I
Why Am I Here?

"Before I formed you in the womb I knew you, before you were born I set you apart; I appointed you as a prophet to the nations." Jeremiah 1:5 (NIV)

My whole life, I knew I was different. I never really fit in anywhere. In some ways I feel like I was here before or that I was meant to be in a time in the past. I'm not sure but I know I was sent here for something bigger than me.

I listened to other kids my age talk and realized what they said was very different from the things I wanted, the things I thought about, and the things in my heart. In fact, I often found myself drawn to the conversations of my elders. I loved hearing their stories and adventures. I found so much joy in spending time with them and just sitting at their feet.

In the 7th grade, I told my mother that I wanted to be normal. I wanted to be like everyone else. She looked me straight in the eye, and she told me to suck it up. That I wasn't like everybody else. For a moment I was taken aback. It sounded so rough. It didn't sound like my mother.

Then she softened her voice and told me that God had great plans for my life. She told me that I would do great things. She said I was a world changer and that's why I could never be normal. This sounded more like my mother.

My whole life, she was the one holding up the light to show me the way. She was always the one reminding me of my purpose, even before I was fully aware what my purpose was. It would be many years later before I fully understood who I was and why I was here.

One day during a service at Grace Community Church in Greenwood, SC, I had a real awakening. During an altar call led by Evangelist Tracey Stewart,

I received a word that changed my life. Hundreds of people went to the altar that day. I had been up for prayer many times, but this one was different.

As soon as Tracey began to pray for me, she stepped back and proclaimed these words to me. "More than anyone here, you have been gifted with the ability to lift the heads of the brokenhearted, to heal those that are hurting. And you stand here wondering if you are qualified to do this great work. God called you. That qualifies you. There is a time of preparation coming. It's going to be like you have gone away with God, and this is the time He will seal the work and send you out. Don't be afraid."

It was like she had been in my head...read my mail, as many say about prophecies. Later I would find the scripture she referenced. It would become the focus of my life's work, the real and sure purpose of my life.

"The Spirit of the Lord God is upon Me, because the Lord has anointed Me To preach good tidings to the poor; He has

sent Me to heal the brokenhearted, To proclaim liberty to the captives, And the opening of the prison to those who are bound." Isaiah 61:1 (NKJV)

Everything changed that day. I was on my way to living a life full of purpose.

Why are we here? We've all heard that question, maybe asking it of ourselves or even God. Many people spend their whole lives trying to figure this out. They search the whole world over for the answer that can ultimately only be found within.

It is part of the work of our lives to discover what our purpose is. One of the reasons I developed the Purpose Driven Living workshop -- and that I am now writing this book -- is to assist you on that journey so that you spend less time searching and more time doing what you were sent here to do. Why are you here?

_____

_____

_____

_____

_____

_____

_____

_____

_____

_____

_____

Introduction Part II
Chasing Sunshine

"For I know the plans I have for you," declares the Lord, "plans to prosper you and not to harm you, plans to give you hope and a future." Jeremiah 29:11 (NIV)

Many people ask how I got the name Sunshine. Most think it is my given name. But by birth I am Regina Elizabeth. While teaching math at Piedmont Technical College (PTC) in Greenwood, SC, I had a student start calling me Sunshine. When I asked him why, he said, "You're like sunshine. Everything is better when you are around." I thought it was sweet, but I didn't think much about it. As he started calling me Sunshine, others heard him, and they started to call me that too. Soon it spread like wildfire.

It was hard for me to embrace the name

though. Calling myself Sunshine seemed like I was edifying myself and putting myself on a pedestal. I ran from the name until I had a life-changing conversation with my son, Gabriel. He told me I couldn't keep running from who I was. He said that the name Sunshine simply personified my purpose in the earth and that it was what people responded to. Gabriel reminded me that my purpose was to reach others, and if they were drawn to the name, it would give me an opportunity to impact their lives. It's always interesting when the child you've always ministered into now is ministering to you. So, I had to embrace it, and today it's my brand.

When I look back now, I see how perfectly the name Sunshine fits with my purpose to leave people better than I find them. If I can bring a little sunshine into the dark places of someone's life and they begin to see better for themselves, I've done my part. And I just want to do my part and hear, "Well done."

I spent most of my life before age 35 chasing after the life I knew I was meant for, looking for the prize of doing what I was created to do. I found her when I found Sunshine. Everything in my past now made sense -- all the oddities of my personality and how I was so different from those around me. For the first time, I began to feel truly comfortable in my own skin. I knew who I was and why I was here. I caught her. I found Sunshine.

Many of you are trying to find your way. You don't know what your purpose is or why you were sent here. You find yourself searching for the answer to all the questions that keep you up at night.

But you know what? The great thing is that **your purpose is already inside you**. And here's another truth: the challenging thing is also that your purpose is already inside you. LOL. You must dig within to discover what has been with you all the time. Then you must find a way to live in it daily.

This book is the summary of my coaching. It is my method to finding and living your purpose. I have used this process to help many people discover and live their purpose. Here I set out 10 purpose finding questions that you must answer for yourself. If you pay attention, you will begin to see a common thread through all of them that will point to something you are already doing or that will help lead you to the place you are supposed to be.

Once you know for sure why you are here and what your assignment is, let this book be the constant reminder of who you are. The circumstances of your life may change, and you may even change, but your purpose remains the same. God knew everything you would face in this life, and He still gave you the assignment He did.

Are you ready to get started? Let's Go! Start here by writing the questions you have about your life.

_____

_____

_____

_____

_____

_____

_____

_____

_____

_____

_____

_____

_____

_____

_____

_____

_____

Chapter 1: What Do You Love?

"And let us consider how we may spur one another on toward love and good deeds..." Hebrews 10:24 (NIV)

There was a time I would ask people the same question wherever I went: "What is your dream?" I found that question stumped many and left most people speechless. I thought my questions would awaken the dream and purpose inside of people. Instead, my question was getting me nowhere with them.

It wasn't long before I came up with the follow-up question, "What do you love?" This question was almost always met with a smile, a twinkle in their eyes and an answer that flowed out of them. Many of us can very easily tell you who and what we love: our families, our favorite hobbies, etc.

This first question on the journey to Chasing

You is the foundation for this whole journey. God created each of us uniquely to fulfill a purpose in the Earth. He installed within us a love for things directly related to why we are here.

Think about it. We all know teachers or childcare workers who absolutely love kids. You see it all over them when they speak about their work, and you see it when they are spending time with children.

When I answered this question for myself, I said that I love people. I love helping people. I love seeing people win and live their best lives. I love helping people find their way from darkness to the light. One of my favorite things is to be working with someone and see the light come on in their eyes. Those are my best days. I also love math and teaching. I love coaching and public speaking. There is something about getting to share my thoughts, feelings, insights, and ideas with an individual or a group and seeing it impact them in a positive way. It makes me feel alive. I have to admit, it can be draining at times but it lights me up!

I remember coaching a young lady once about a career change that she needed to make. She shared with me that she cried every day before going into her job as a schoolteacher. I told her straight up, "This ain't the job for you. You know it, and those kids know it. Figure out what you love and get out."

She said that she really loved the volunteer work she was doing with the elderly at a local assisted living facility. I told her to immediately start looking at openings at that facility and others like it. I also encouraged her to get additional training in this field. I told her that it would take some real effort on her part but that it would be the difference between spending her life doing something she enjoyed or living in misery. The choice was hers.

I remember the sense of relief she experienced as we had this conversation. No one had ever told her it was okay to find a way to make money doing something you love. She acted as if I had given her a winning lottery ticket.

I've told many people that if you can find a way

to make money doing what you love, you get to do something you love every day and people pay you to enjoy your life. It's real. I live this every day. I promise you it is worth the time, effort, and chances you gotta take to live a life you love.

Recognizing what I love has been a game changer for me. So, pause now and look at yourself and your life. **What do you love**? What do you love to do? What would you do for free if money was no object? What activities bring you the most joy? When you answer this question, you begin to awaken the purpose in your life. God created you as the answer to a problem, and at the same time, He created you to love being in that space.

_____

_____

_____

_____

_____

_____

_____

_____

_____

_____

_____

_____

Chapter 2: What Do You See?

"But blessed are your eyes because they see, and your ears because they hear." Matthew 13: 16 (NIV)

When I lived in Greenwood, SC, I attended Grace Community Church under the leadership of Pastors Rod and Carmen Schultz. This is the place where my gifts were honed and crafted before I launched out into the world as Regina Sunshine.

One Sunday morning, Pastor Rod had the ushers pass out a 5 by 7 notecard to everyone in the service. He explained to us that for the next week we needed to make note of the things we see in the world, the things that seem to show up over and over during our day.

For that next week, I noted that everywhere I went I saw hurting people...sad people, lonely people,

people distraught or upset. They were everywhere. I remember that my son Gabriel told me he saw division amongst people, division across the races, socioeconomics, etc.

On the next Sunday morning, Pastor Rod asked a few people to share what they saw while completing his assignment. Then he revealed why he had us to do this exercise. He explained that we all see different things as we walk through the world because what we see is tied to our purpose in the earth. We see challenges and problems that we are sent here and divinely equipped to address.

I looked at my notecard. I immediately went back to what Tracey Stewart said to me at the altar that day. The reason I saw hurting people is because I'm an encourager, a lover of people. I have been sent here to love and encourage those who need it, to help heal those who are broken, to help lift their heads. When I thought about my son, I could see why he saw division. He is a connector. He connects people. He bridges gaps and brings people together.

Many things began to make sense after that day. Why I seemed to walk into every situation and find the same problem to fix. Why I was drawn to whoever was sad or needed a hug. Why when I walked into a room it seemed like a spotlight was over the head of whoever was hurt or broken. I was sent here to love and encourage these people.

We all have different purposes. It's ok if you don't understand why one person is so passionate about saving the whales and someone else about feeding the homeless or another about littering, and it doesn't make sense to you. It doesn't have to make sense to you. It's not a part of your purpose. Because as Dr. Deborah Houston told me, "Every good work is not God's work for you."

God allows us to see things through the eyes of our purpose. You can walk into a room with a group of friends, and you will all see very different things according to the purpose for which you were created. This is why it's important that everyone finds their lane and stays in their lane. If everyone is doing their part, fulfilling their purpose, all the needs will be met.

Now it's your turn. For the next 5-7 days, take notes in your phone or a notebook or on a notecard and answer Question Number 2, **What Do You See** throughout your day. Record it here and begin to reflect on what these things say about you. You will notice that you may even see some things that remind you of your answer to Question Number 1, What Do You Love?

_____

_____

_____

_____

_____

_____

_____

_____

_____

_____

_____

_____

_____

_____

_____

smart, passionate, and inspiring. I didn't want to say a word because I just wanted to listen to him talk. The more I learned about him, the more I wanted to be just like him. From that day, he became my brother, and he is someone I always look to for counsel and a good word.

You are inspired by kindred spirits, like minds, like hearts because your work and purpose are tied to theirs. You are a continuation of what they have begun, and as they move on, the torch is passed to you. So, my 3rd Question is, **Who inspires you?** What characteristics do they possess that you admire?

_____

_____

_____

_____

_____

_____

_____

_____

_____

_____

_____

_____

_____

_____

_____

Chapter 4: What Are You Good At?

"There are different kinds of gifts, but the same Spirit distributes them." I Corinthians 12:4 (NIV)

All of my life I have been gifted in the areas of public speaking, writing, math, tutoring, and working with people. These are things that don't require much thought or preparation for me, and I LOVE doing them. When I was younger, I never really thought about how these gifts, talents, and abilities impacted my life's purpose. But now I know they are directly related. The things that you love and can do with ease can be arrows pointing you in the direction of your life's work or career.

I went to college for Chemical Engineering. Why? My high school chemistry teacher Mr. Clontz said, "You are great in chemistry and math. You should be a chemical engineer." At that time,

Chemical Engineers were the highest paid bachelors degree coming out of college. And I saw dollar signs.

Even though I was aware that I was different and had heard my whole life I would do something great, I never once considered any of that when choosing a college major. I went off to attend North Carolina A&T in August of 1990. By my sophomore year, I knew engineering wasn't for me. I decided to change my major to Business.

I remember calling my mom from the dorm pay phone, excited that I thought I knew what I wanted to do. When I told her my new plan, she told me to call her when I felt better. Now, my mother is one of the most positive and supportive people you can meet. Although her response seemed harsh, she went on to explain. She reminded me that I was in college on an engineering scholarship which was free money. She told me that I could always get my MBA after taking advantage of the opportunity to complete my undergraduate degree for free. I understood what she meant and agreed to stay where I was.

Fast forward to right after college, my college boyfriend and I had a son. Soon after, we married. Going back to get my MBA was a distant thought as now I was fully immersed in my life as wife and mother. Years later when my son was in preschool, I had the opportunity to go and tutor at Piedmont Technical College in Greenwood, SC. I absolutely loved my time with the students because, as I said before, I love tutoring and math.

While tutoring at Piedmont Tech, the head of the math department, Sherry Holland, asked me to teach a math class. She said that she had heard so many positive things from the students I tutored that it occurred to her I might like to teach a class. Now, at first I said, "NO!" LOL. I had never ever wanted to be a teacher. But Sherry persisted and finally made me this offer. "Come and teach one class. If you don't like it, I will never ask you again." I agreed and that one decision changed my life. I walked into that classroom the first day, and I felt like the Energizer Bunny. It was like someone flipped the switch in my back and I was on. I loved every moment.

In the classroom, I found a convergence of what I love, what I see in the word, who inspires me, and what I was naturally good at. Teaching. Years later when I began empowerment coaching and classes, my love for teaching was combined with my direct love and ability to inspire and encourage others. I am forever grateful that Sherry Holland didn't give up on me. Through my connection to her, I experienced game changing moments in my life.

So Question 4, **What are you naturally good at**? What are the gifts, talents, and abilities that flow effortlessly from you? What do people always ask you to do because you excel at it? Your answers to these questions will help you identify projects, work, and career moves that are tied to your purpose.

_____

_____

_____

_____

_____

_____

_____

_____

_____

_____

_____

_____

_____

_____

_____

Chapter 5: What Would You Teach?

"We have different gifts, according to the grace given to each of us. If your gift is prophesying, then prophesy in accordance with your faith; if it is serving, then serve; if it is teaching, then teach." Romans 12:6-7 (NIV)

I heard someone say once that all of us are teachers. I didn't always believe that, but the pandemic and down time of 2020 showed me otherwise. It was interesting that once people had time to be still, so many realized that they had valuable content inside themselves. As a result, we saw a record number of new podcasts, YouTube channels, online courses, and the like being created. Even working with my Empowerment Coaching clients, I began to discover that each of us has information that someone else needs, considers valuable, and is willing to pay to access.

For me, teaching comes naturally. I didn't know that before I took the Math Instructor job at PTC. But after that, I began to recognize all the ways I was teaching. From helping the girls at A Place for Us Ministries get their GEDs to leading empowerment sessions with Destinys Daughters of Promise, I kept walking into and looking for opportunities to teach.

Along with that, others were asking me to teach. In everyday settings or in business situations, people were always asking me to take on the role of teaching. I could not get away from it. But before Sherry Holland asked me to teach, I never considered teaching as a possibility for my life.

What's even more interesting is that when I looked at my life, I had always been teaching or tutoring math. Even as a middle school student, I had adults in my hometown of Tabor City, NC ask my parents if I could assist them with their college math homework. Then I tutored all through high school and college. And as I mentioned before, I was tutoring at PTC when Sherry Holland found me and asked me to teach.

The other thing I found interesting is that these opportunities to teach always led back to things I love. For instance, I love math, and I started teaching math. I love helping people so my time volunteering at different charities made sense. I found when I was teaching something I loved, it wasn't work at all.

Our purpose is always there. It is a common thread that weaves throughout our lives. Sometimes we just need someone to cause us to pause and ask us the right questions. It's never far. We just have to wake up and see it.

So, what is your answer to Question 5, **What would you teach**? Does it relate to any of your answers from the previous chapters?

_____

_____

_____

_____

_____

_____

_____

_____

_____

_____

_____

_____

_____

_____

_____

_____

_____

Chapter 6: What Would You Regret?

"I have fought the good fight, I have finished the race, I have kept the faith." II Timothy 4:7 (NIV)

When we look at our lives as a whole, we all have those items -- be they Bucket List or otherwise -- that we know we have to do. There are things we dream about. There are those things that we just know must be a part of our lives. Whether it is due to fear, not feeling prepared, not receiving support, or whatever else, you know that if you don't do it, you will spend your life wondering "what if"? Sometimes it is better to do something and fail and learn than to avoid doing it at all.

In 2017, I started my own production studio. It was hard work. I partnered with some extraordinary people to create something I dreamed out. I had so many ideas for expansion as well as ways to pitch some of our shows to major networks and streaming platforms. In 2021, I had to shut that studio down. There are times I felt like a failure because of that. But I know I would have regretted it if I had never started my studio.

I met some truly amazing people during my time running my studio. I had some incredible moments and life-changing experiences there. I learned a lot about myself and being a business owner. It was hard, but it forced me to dig deep and grow in ways that I am not sure I would have without it. I am thankful I did it, and now it is not on my list of things I regret not doing.

When I look over my life, I know there are some things I am glad I did, things that I know I would regret if I didn't do them. Some I was successful at. Some I failed. But I would have regretted it if I had not taken the chance. As you begin to think about your life in its entirety, are there things that you know you will regret if you don't do them?

So, now answer Question 6, **What would you**

regret not doing, being or having in your life?

_____

_____

_____

_____

_____

_____

_____

_____

_____

_____

_____

_____

_____

_____

Chapter 7: What Matters Most?

"God saved you by his grace when you believed. And you can't take credit for this; it is a gift from God. Salvation is not a reward for the good things we have done, so none of us can boast about it." Ephesians 2:8-9 (NLT)

As I look back over my life now, I can already see there are things I want to do by the end of my life. With each year that passes, there is an urgency to get things done and make sure I die empty. These thoughts lead to re-evaluating where I am and seeing what is next.

This question immediately makes me think of the projects that are on my heart that I've either started and stopped or that haven't made their way out of my head. The thought of reaching 90 years old and those ideas still being in my heart and not making it to full manifestation scares me.

To live the life I dream of and truly be happy, I must see these things through. I dream of an Awesome Girl School where girls are taught to seek purpose in their career pursuits. I see a community center/business co-sharing space that also has a studio for creating podcasts and talk shows. My dreams are of major award shows where we honor those that are doing grassroots work and affecting lasting change. I see a bookshelf of books in the Awesome Girl Book series and hundreds of girls that have added "published author" to their resumes and college applications. I envision a picture of a group of girls who have either gotten full scholarships to their dream college or funding to start their own businesses. I know there will be many shows that we produce that are on many different streaming and major platforms. All of these things matter to me and so many more.

Another major part of who I am is love. Love will be at the center of my story. My love for people is the foundation of everything I do. So, love will be woven through every project and milestone. I see love everywhere at every turn. I want to have it in all parts of my life. I know I will be married to the love of my life, and we will be spending our days traveling and living life together on purpose. That matters to me.

Imagine this, you are now 90 years old, sitting on a rocking chair outside on your porch; you can feel the spring breeze gently brushing against your face. You are blissful and happy and are pleased with the wonderful life with which you've been blessed. Looking back at your life and all that you've achieved and acquired, all the relationships you've developed, answer Question 7…**What matters to you most?** List them out.

_____

_____

_____

_____

_____

_____

_____

Chapter 8: What Causes Do You Believe In?

"Remember this: Whoever sows sparingly will also reap sparingly, and whoever sows generously will also reap generously. Each of you should give what you have decided in your heart to give, not reluctantly or under compulsion, for God loves a cheerful giver." II Corinthians 9:6-7 (NIV)

You can tell a lot about a person by where they spend their money and their time. And you can definitely find your way into knowing someone's heart by knowing the causes or charities they support or that tug at their heart. When searching to discover your purpose, taking time to examine who and what you believe in and support will give you an even greater window into why you are here.

My heart sings for most things related to helping people, but I find that issues that involve girls and women are my passion. I've spent my life volunteering at women's shelters, for girls' mentoring organizations, group homes, and all types of events and workshops that assist girls and women. It's where I'm naturally drawn. It wasn't until I fully understood my purpose that I began to recognize that everything that I was pulled to do were all related to the same areas of concern, girls and women.

When it comes to making donations of money or time, organizations like Mercy Ministries, St. Jude's Hospital, and Kenneth Copeland Ministries have been on top of my list. Others like MEGS House, A Place for Us Ministries, and the like have been where I gave more of myself.

When you look at the nonprofit organizations and causes around you, which ones tug at your heart? What fundraisers are you compelled to give to without hesitation? What areas are you willing to donate your time and energy to bless? These areas are a part of you, and this is why they call out to you. When you understand this and look within, your purpose will begin to unfold.

If you look back over the questions we've already covered, I'm guessing that you are seeing a common theme...of course you are. You are uncovering your purpose. So, here's Question 8, **What causes do you strongly believe in or connect with?**

_____

_____

_____

_____

_____

_____

_____

_____

_____

_____

_____

_____

Chapter 9: What Would Your Message Be?

"Whoever brings blessing will be enriched, and one who waters will himself be watered." Proverbs 11:25 (ESV)

I've had many opportunities to speak in front of audiences of all sizes. Most times I'm given a topic, but sometimes I get to choose what I want to talk about. I find that when given the opportunity, I often choose to speak about Self Worth/Self Image, Finding Purpose, Creating a Positive Mindset or Pursuing your Dreams. All of these topics are very dear to me. They all tie directly to my heart and what I love to help people with.

The work I do in Empowerment Coaching, teaching, motivational speaking, and girls' empowerment are all tied to these topics. They show up in everything that I do. I can't run from them. They come up in conversations I have with others. Even when I'm just being a regular person in my regular life, I find myself sharing this info and trying to help others.

Every message has an audience. Sometimes the message is the purpose, and sometimes the audience is. Sometimes you are passionate about the message, and sometimes it's just something that weighs on your heart. The message can be layered or very simple. Whatever the message is, it is a clue to your purpose…your calling.

When you know what the message is, it helps lead you to what's next. For some, it can be the journey to a deeper place and that message is speaking to just you when you thought it was for others. Whatever the direction the message takes you, it will help lead you to why you are here.

So, what are you always looking to talk about or share? What do you try to teach others? What comes naturally out of you in conversations. These are all clues to why you are here and the work you are supposed to be doing.

If you could get a message across to a large group of people, who would those people be? Question 9: **What would your message be?**

_____

_____

_____

_____

_____

_____

_____

_____

_____

_____

_____

_____

_____

_____

_____

_____

_____

Chapter 10: How Could You Help?

"Do nothing out of selfish ambition or vain conceit. Rather, in humility value others above yourselves, 4 not looking to your own interests but each of you to the interests of the others."
Philippians 2:3-4 (NIV)

I've been blessed in my life to work with people who have helped me in this area. I have always looked for ways to serve and share my gifts. That is naturally who I am and what I do. I have always looked for organizations and situations to volunteer to use my gifts and talents.

Then as I progressed through life, I've met some truly amazing people who helped direct me to even be more proficient. My former business coach Lynita Mitchell-Blackwell was one of those people. She was able to look at me and what I had already done then see how I could direct my efforts more efficiently. The blessing was that she showed me how to do those things and get paid.

In the time I've known her, I've gone from being an employee for someone else to working fulltime in my own purpose driven work. I'm an Empowerment Coach. I started a girls empowerment organization called the Awesome Girl Academy. I operate a thriving math tutoring business. Many times throughout the year I am invited to be a Keynote speaker. I have hosted my own talk show, *The Regina Sunshine Show*, where I get to reach people globally with the messages I have discussed throughout this book. Every day I get to do things I love, the things I was purposed to do, and people pay me. These are things I would do anyway for free, and my coach showed me how to create an income with them.

I'm not saying that everyone has to turn their passion into a career. I'm just letting you know that it's possible. Maybe you explore those things during your free time outside of work. The important thing is this: You must find a way to tap into why you are here.

Your life takes on a whole other thing when you find a way for your purpose to be a part of your everyday life.

What was put in you must come out of you. You were created for this purpose to find its way out of you. You have to be who you were sent here to be. Given your talents, passions, and values, ask yourself Question 10, **How could you use these resources to help, to serve, to contribute** (to people, beings, causes, organization, environment, planet, etc.)?

_____

_____

_____

_____

_____

_____

_____

_____

_____

_____

_____

_____

_____

_____

_____

Chapter 11: 27 Days

"And we know that all things work together for good to those who love God, to those who are the called according to His purpose." Romans 8:28 (NKJV)

27 Days. My mother died on November 17, 2022. Then my father died on December 14, 2022 -- 27 days later. In 27 days, my entire life turned upside down. Everything I thought I knew for sure was in question. In 27 days, I went from Regina Sunshine to questioning who I was. In 27 days, I went from a life of certainty to feeling lost and alone. 27 Days.

I stopped going to events and really doing anything beyond the day-to-day required activities. When opportunities to participate in projects or activities arose, sometimes it was a straight no. Sometimes I would mention invitations to my sister Pam, and she would just say no. She knows where I have been and that I've felt like I had nothing to give…no Sunshine for anyone.

Then I had to attend an event for an organization called DDP, Destiny's Daughters of Promise. I am their lead workshop facilitator, and I also lead their virtual Middle School and High School Girls Empowerment Session. I only attended because my baby sister Zoe was enrolled in the program, and as a senior, she was to speak and to receive a scholarship. I told the founder that I would possibly be there, but although I was on the program to speak, I would not take the stage. It would be the first event I had attended since before my parents passed.

At the event, one of the Workshop speakers was giving her background and mentioned she was a grief coach. Everything she said that day sounded like she was there just for me. During her talk, she mentioned just doing one deliberate thing that moved you in the direction of finding yourself again. At that moment, I decided to attend an event. And then at the end of the event when I was recognized with the other facilitators, although I refused to go on stage, at the last moment I asked for the mic and did affirmations with the attendees. Why? Because it's who I am.

About 3 weeks later, right after the DDP Event, I had my first dream about my mother since she passed. I don't remember much, but these words she spoke to me, "You know who you are."

So many times in my life, my mother told me that God had great purpose for my life, that I was set a part to do great things. She told me that any time I enter a room, the atmosphere would shift because I was there. She told me I was a world changer. Because of her, I have always known who I was and that gave me strength and power to be who I was in the earth.

So much of what she poured into me is how I am the Regina Sunshine many people know. Beyond that, it impacted how I raised my son and speak into his life. And I began to hear my own words to him encouraging me. I have often said, "Gabriel, God knew every challenge you would face, everything you would encounter, and He still gave you the purpose and assignment that He did."

I am reminded that God knew every challenge I am facing and all the pain I would be feeling, and my assignment hasn't changed. Here's what I know for sure. I am who God says I am. I can do what God says I can do. I can have what God says I can have.

From my heart to yours…know this. You are who God says you are. You can do what God says you can do. You can have what God says you can have. He knew everything you would face in this life, and He still filled your life with purpose. When the world looks dark and it's hard to shine, hold on to Who and What you know to be true.

The last speaking engagement I had before my mother passed was a women's conference at my home church. My mother had rallied hard for me to be the keynote speaker, and I was. It was a dream come true for her and for me. To minister in the same place where I was saved and to have the person, my mother, that got me started speaking in attendance, is a moment I will always remember.

In 27 days, my life changed forever but what didn't change is who I am and what I've been called to do. Know this…I'm still here. There's still purpose in my life. I'm still winning.

_____

_____

_____

_____

_____

_____

_____

_____

_____

_____

_____

_____

_____

_____

_____

_____

Chapter 12: Broken But Still Whole

"In the same way, let your light shine before others, that they may see your good deeds and glorify your Father in heaven."
Matthew 5:16 (NIV)

I watched Kirk Franklin's documentary *Father's Day*. In that film, he stated that he had only ever known himself broken, and he wondered who he would have been whole. In other words, he had lived his whole life from a broken place because he had experienced so much trauma. When we think of people who have experienced some of the things he did, we think of people who have faced so much that they live lives that are hard and not full of the accomplishments Kirk Franklin has made. But Kirk has lived an extraordinarily successful life and has helped a lot of people through his gifts.

Without the pain of his childhood, would Kirk

Franklin still accomplish the same things he did? Would he achieve less, or would he achieve more? Did the pain make him push harder? Was the music born out of the pain or in spite of it? We will never know.

We can't operate from those unknowns. What we can access is that what may have looked broken about his life, created a whole lot of help and healing for others.

When I look at who I was before my parents died, it is like someone I once knew or someone from another life. I have to admit that at times I have been afraid that I would never be who I once was.

I have felt so broken that I wondered if I would ever be whole. But after watching Kirk's documentary, it occurred to me that my brokenness can still bring much help and healing to others.

I have experienced things that made me feel like I was losing my mind. And at the same time, I am still here. My purpose is what keeps me sane and moving forward. It's the very thing that has helped me Find My Way Back to the Light. To those watching I may appear broken, but when it comes to my purpose, I am always whole.

I do not have all the answers, but I know that when all else fails and the world is spinning, you have to hold on to what is fixed and sure. God is the same yesterday, today, and forever. He placed a purpose inside you having full knowledge of everything about you and everything you would face. So, when everything is moving, your purpose is a safe place to land.

This is why it is so important to ask all the questions and do all the work to discover your purpose. When something unexpected or life changing occurs, you have a home to return to that offers a safe place to operate from.

I hope me sharing my journey will help you on yours. I was Chasing Sunshine, and I caught her. I hope you catch who you are chasing, and when everything turns upside down, you will hold on to it as you Find Your Way Back To The Light.

Dear Reader,

I hope my stories and struggles will help you to identify your own. The journey is not easy, but it is necessary. Once you know your purpose, it will give you something to hold on to when everything around you is moving.

I pray that you find all of your answers, and they lead you to the solutions you need for your life. You are still here and that means there's still time. And when you are ready, write me and tell me how it is going. I am excited to hear your story.

Be blessed. Keep Winning!
Regina Sunshine

Personal Scripture Affirmations

I was created in the image of God.
Greater is He that is within me than he that is in the world.
I will praise thee; for I am fearfully and wonderfully made.
I am more than a conqueror through Him that loves me.
I can do all things through Christ who strengthens me.
If God is for me, who can be against me.
God has not given me a spirit of fear, but of power, and love and a sound mind.
I am the temple of the Holy Spirit and the Spirit of God dwells in me.
I am worthy of the call God has on my life.
I am worthy of living the life I was created for.
I am worthy of the dreams God has placed in my heart.
I Am Worthy.

Personal General Affirmations

I was born to win.

I am more than a conqueror.

I was created for greatness.

I was born to be victorious.

I will achieve my dreams.

I can be anything I choose.

I can do anything I set my mind to.

I am a champion.

I am worthy of the best things in life.

I am worthy of the dreams in my heart.

I am worthy of living a great life.

I am worthy.

Partner Affirmations

God loves you just the way you are.

You are beautiful because you were created in love.

You were fearfully and wonderfully made.

You have the seeds of greatness within you.

You were born to live a victorious life.

You are brilliant, gorgeous, talented, and fabulous.

You Are Worthy.

About the Author

Regina Sunshine Robinson is an Empowerment Specialist who focuses on writing, publishing, motivational speaking, coaching, and consulting. She is the CEO of Regina Sunshine Global Network. Regina Sunshine is a graduate of North Carolina A&T State University with a Bachelor of Science in Chemical Engineering. She is an award-winning author, talk show host, and community activist. Regina is the author of a book on developing a positive mental attitude entitled *Regina Sunshine State of Mind*. She also contributed to the *Chicken Soup for the Soul* editions *Curvy & Confident* and *Be You*. She is a lover of people and servant to God's people. Her personal motto is "It's Not Over Til I Win," and she wins when she sees others winning.

Get this title, also from Author Regina Sunshine Robinson.

REGINA "SUNSHINE" ROBINSON